EX CATHEDRA

XXV

PETER JOANNIDES

Printed in the United States of America
Corrected second printing, 2019

ISBN 978-0-9892536-8-0

www.PetroulisI@gmail.com

AUTHOR'S NOTE

This is the latest in a series of **Ex Cathedras** begun in 1972. The first eight are embedded in my major work **Amán Amán! Ex Cathedras (IX-XV)** and **More Ex Cathedras (XVI-XXII)** were published in two separate volumes, followed by the additional separate publication of **Ex Cathedra XXIII** and **Ex Cathedra XXIV**.

Peter Joannides

ALSO BY PETER JOANNIDES

Amán Amán!
Ex Cathedras (IX-XV)
Ex Cathedras (XVI-XXII)
Ex Cathedra XXIII
Ex Cathedra XXIV

December 1, 2015

Ex

Cathedra

25th
Encyclical

von Herrn Doktor Professor Peter Joannides

1

The best retsina is **varelísia** retsina, closely followed by the bottled CAIR retsina of Rhodos.

2

When I die, I don't want it to be when it's dark.

I don't at all mind the sunlight.

Even if I were to have a relationship with Maria Houkli, I would be terribly intimidated by her well-spoken Greek.

4

It'd be nice to see CNN's Dana Bash and John King get back together.

Intellectual titans don't faze me, since I'm one of them.

6

I saw the original of **An Affair to Remember**, and I thought it was shamelessly encroaching upon my original.

7

If ever there was a movie that did so much with so little, it was Dennis Weaver and **Duel**.

8

I'm such a mass of contradictions and repetitions, I'm a mess.

9

All my life I've been expected to conform to one thing or another, in one way or another.

I no longer conform to anything except what will keep me breathing and keep me out of jail.

As bad as football is, I'd rather watch a football game over a basketball game, anytime.

11

Basketball has to be the sloppiest game there is.

Google has made everything easy and unsurprising.

A Lackawanna 16356 moment:

One cool, sweatered morning in Asmara, getting ready for the down and round and round and down trek to sweltering Massawa.

14

China's rise.

That was quick! It caught me when I wasn't looking.

Oh all those advertising executives and brainstormers, oh how they must think of themselves as so so clever.

16

Just about everybody's handwriting is better than mine.

Daydream

I win the Nobel Prize.

I ask (retired) President Obama if he would give my acceptance speech.

He accepts.

I allow him to speak for seven minutes (not a second more) before his delivery, at which time he is free to say anything he wishes about any matter, including that he disagrees with what I am about to say.

He delivers my rather brief speech.

The speech is about the need for a dictatorial Planetary Authority, to be vested in **ONE** man with powers unrescindable except under extraordinary circumstances. A man benevolent, informed, and scientifically oriented with a vision of what this planet could be like. (A man much younger than myself.) A man who will obviously have to delegate, but who will ultimately make the important decisions. A man who will no doubt make mistakes, but be eminently capable of reversing himself. A man who will bequeath his powers and responsibilities to his chosen successor.

That it behooves the human community to find, anoint, and protect this man as soon as possible.

Before it is too late.

The best hot dogs in the world, better than all the bratwursts, bockwursts, bregenwursts, kochwursts, what-have-you...

Cypriot **loukánika**.

Doctors have become so streamlined these days.

Don't astronomers realize that The World is much bigger than The Universe?

21

It takes a single somebody to tell everyone else that something is good; and then everyone else signs on.

22

Who knows? If I live another 50 years, I might even turn into a Republican.

Turner Classic Movies

My God, how dated, transparent, predictable, and a little bit ridiculous some of those old films are.

20

E.g., Donald Duck is not the same as the physical causes and correlates of Donald Duck.

Thinkers, moralists, philosophers…, from times long past, have always tried to **REDUCE** everything to one set of principles or another.

Why don't they just give it up.

Dear Cratylus,

We're getting there, slowly but surely, inevitably, we're getting there…

Hard science (medicine, chemistry, electronics…).

The rest is mostly blather.

When one finds other people's religions a bit silly, shouldn't it cross his mind that his may be silly as well?

23

Not, however, Jean Arthur and Cary Grant in **Only Angels Have Wings**.

The **when** of what is read, heard, seen is essential and undisentangleable from the what.

I can't help it:

There is a general alienness about the French.

And a definite **Heimweh** about Italians.

Adam Gopnik

Wouldn't you know it? Couldn't you have guessed it?

A Francophile.

It has taken me so long to realize that my audience is hardly anyone I know.

There's a certain self-congratulating, formula-ridden, first-and-a-half-rateness and sassy ungenuineness about a goodly number of **New Yorker** staff writers.

35

Hume was dead right about the self.

How can you compare Greek music and American music!

Greek music is mostly beautiful; American music is mostly crap.

37

Don't you sometimes just know, even without hearing the niceties, that the conversation at the next table is little more than garbage.

I was once a scaredy-cat kid without much assertiveness or courage.

39

All that targeted vituperation and vitriol all these years.

Maybe it was just the Southern accent itself, and not much else, that was responsible all along.

Didn't I once say that much can be laid at the doorstep of Aesthetics?

I would do an ad for American Express for free.

I wouldn't do an Alpo ad for $1,000,000.

I guess I've made it **ad nauseam** clear that I detest ads, **ANY** and **ALL** ads.

I guess this maybe makes me some sort of communist.

Everyone comes up through the ranks, except Athena and me.

44

When you take a dislike to someone, try to get hold of some of his early photos, and the dislike will be greatly ameliorated.

If I were running things, it would have to be behind the scenes.

I want no part of any ceremonies.

I can tell that something is an ad within ½ to 1 second after exposure.

Doesn't this intimate something? Doesn't this tell you something?

"Tergiversate" is an odd word.

"Iconic" is a pretentious word.

"Mellifluous" is a soothing word.

How Is It?

Rita Hayworth

Well-proportioned, well-endowed, sultry, teasy, provocative…

Yet I, not in the least bit attracted.

49

What a colossal chunk of my time, life, and energy was given to handball.

I sometimes wonder whether it could have been somewhat more wisely spent.

Mike Huckabee

A pure and unadulterated example of a logorrheic windbag.

51

Miami, Florida: nothing whatever aristocratic about it.

36

Sometimes you have to indulge in hyperbole, in order to make a point.

53

What happened to Moritz Schlick could happen to anyone, in any societal position.

I don't care what the critics said, and I don't care what even the actors themselves who were in it said, I still think **Bright Leaf** was a good film.

Imitation-crab is a sorry imitation of crab.

I'm not sure that men who sport beards and moustaches are all that far removed from jerks who flaunt tattoos.

Spanish Radio Station: I love it when music holds sway; I turn it off as soon as someone starts blabbing.

I always wanted to be a poet of science.

Haunting: The Tigre music of Eritrea.

Instant likes: A good example: Prime Minister Yitzhak Rabin of Israel.

"The American Dream"

What a mostly vapid, vacuous, and self-important phrase, especially from the mouths of latter-day politicians.

Whatever possessed me, once in Rhodos, to try to give a philosophical lecture **in Greek** to a **sophisticated Greek audience**? Probably one of the most foolhardy things I've ever done.

62

Far more so than just **orating** my Ex Cathedra

in Spanish to a college audience in Cartagena.

Day by day, more and more, I'm getting closer and closer to the estate of Stephen Hawking.

65

With so many writers, you're not dealing with a person; you're dealing with a show-off.

I don't get it: What's so great about living in New York?

Six major surgeries: hell of a price to pay for a few handball wins.

I remember the little hand-held pencil sharpener, and the writhy curly shavings that would detach and go wriggling dancing away—so long long ago.

Pain is an absolute.

And there is so terribly much of it, both for humans and animals.

Drugs don't do anything for me, any of them.

I'll even take coffee over any drug.

Alcohol, however, **does** do a whole lot for me.

This author's three-volume Magnum Opus as well as **all** succeeding **Ex Cathedras** should be considered as one indivisible and unfragmented whole.

This is what the author wants, intends, and suggests.

72

Don't worry about what doesn't hurt.

After all these years, rereading my colleague Bill Lee's **Athenian Adventure** about the Greece of 58 years ago. And suddenly realizing, although a bit dated after 58 years, what a well-written book it was, wittily perceptive, impressive in its range of knowledge and reference, erudite without being stuffy, a commendable oeuvre.

And all this time, right under my nose.

To be unable to scratch, a place that **SCREAMS** to be scratched, is one version of hell on earth.

Not long ago, bitter implacable enemies; now, bosom pals:

Japan and the United States; France and Germany; Ireland and Great Britain…

Someone ought to adjust this sort of crappy (and insulting) history.

Where in the world do the networks dig up these androgynous smarty-pants anchors?

I want a President who would spurn the White House National Correspondents' Association Dinner.

It hurts to see someone as intelligent as Obama make a fool of himself.

The Planetary Dictator has neither the time nor the inclination for ceremonies.

Having been laid up for several months with a major surgery, I have spent hours and hours watching Turner Classic Movies, and I am sorry to report a certain sudden insight about actors and acting that took hold—unforced, unexpected, and unannounced—a certain general disillusionment that both saddens and liberates.

Isn't it strange that amidst all these slogans, come-ons, ads, and hype, I would find the Bill and Melinda Gates Foundation statement of purpose so eloquent:

"That all people deserve the chance to live a healthy and productive life."

Enough about Socrates, Plato, Aristotle!

Let's hear about Leucippus, Democritus, Epicurus, Lucretius.

No man loved maps more than I.

I find climbing the Old Man of Hoy in the Orkneys a stupid thing to do.

When I used to lecture, I would bandy about the word "Renaissance" up and down, left and right, as if I, the expert, knew what I was talking about.

How embarrassing it is to think back upon those stagy and impostrous ways.

Guess I must be pretty much of a lowbrow. Neither Art nor Opera nor Modern Dance nor Classical Music nor Sculptures nor Plays… have ever done very much for me.

I wonder where squirrels go when they're about to die?

I wish someone would actually create the SUPER TAPE that I talk about at the beginning of "six martinis" in the Altered States in **Amán Amán!**

One hell of a musical medley!

89

What makes anyone think that a muffled, garbled narration from the inside of scuba paraphernalia adds anything to an undersea documentary.

"Statesmen" who slide their hand in that time-

honored hand-in-vest pose—
                              what a giveaway!

91

There's something about Fred Astaire hoofing it up that mesmerizes and makes for "can't-keep-my-eyes-off-him."

The maker and the making of a documentary should be invisible.

In my vituperative section in **Amán Amán!,** where I rake over the coals all the world's religions and sects, the reader may wonder why there was no mention of Islam.

And the truth is that, at the time, Islam was the furthest thing from my mind. I simply did not think about it.

Now an interesting question that arises is whether, had I thought about it, and given the **present** atmosphere about the matter and what I am **now** aware of, I would have written differently. And the honest answer is that I would have trod more lightly.

But, at the time, had I thought about it, I would have been as merciless about Islam as I was about all the others.

This, then, is the truth.

90

I was thinking of Mustapha Kemal who I would have thought, being the progressive that he was, would have graduated from such a fustian gesture.

95

Teetotalers and vegetarians are missing a lot.

There is such a flabbiness about tourists.

How aware I am now of stumbling and slow-moving elders, of canes, wheelchairs, walkers, handicap stickers and spaces.

48

For some reason, which I don't at all pretend to understand, I think any involvement would have been a form of **incest**.

The   dowager   Victoria   and   her   grandsons,
Imperial Helmeted Cousins and Kin, deciding when and
with whom to wage war—

                          and   thus   having   millions   of
men maimed and killed.

The whole thing makes me sick to my stomach.

What I like about surgery is that, when successful, it solves the problem **wholesale**.

101

I find it hard to believe, and intolerable to accept, that a few autocrats (on whatever side) managed to persuade and mobilize thousands, millions of men to go and slaughter one another.

Sometimes I think that the foremost and overriding concern should have to do with people who are in severe chronic pain.

103

No doubt this has to do with the flimsiest of reason and evidence, but the fact is I like Stefan Zweig more than I do Thomas Mann.

Nurses in a hospital: how friendly, outgoing, smiling, encouraging, do-more-than-her-share some; how pinched, dour, Javert-like, do-the-minimum others.

This from **my** limited experience: All cinema re-makes are inferior to their originals, except for **An Affair to Remember**.

A glass half full of fizzed-out coca-cola, and half full of cold water: not too bad a drink.

107

What a turnabout!

For years and years and years, I hardly ever gave a thought to the workings of my body.

Now, it's all I can do to keep it together.

Philosophers have always been amused by scientificos who claim that black is not a color.

109

Lotto was the only way for **me** to get ahead.

I had no interest in any other career path.

Judy Woodruff

Once I tried to flirt with her when she visited Jacksonville University with fellow journalist Garrick Utley.

Later, I called her "a straw-filled Sunday School teacher" and dropped her from my "Cavett list."

Now, I think she is, and always has been, an exemplar professional lady.

111

No matter how full and belly-bursting a lunch may be, by nightfall hunger will once again set in.

Ages ago, when in my vituperative mood I blasted and excoriated the U.S. Marines, I was thinking of their "starched and spotless uniforms" with "shiny buttons" and "red-striped pants," of the parades, formations, salutes and drills, patriotic sonorities...

I was not thinking of them in combat.

113

I am from another time and another clime and am carried aloft by this modern world, hanging on as best I can.

Old Age and Deterioration

If I weren't a part of it, I'd probably observe it with considerable interest.

Is it conceivable (logically possible) for a new color to suddenly appear that is as different from all the known colors as green is different from blue?

My erstwhile Paper on Sex

As long as no childbirth is involved, or disease, or coercion, or pain (both physical and psychological), then **anything goes**.

It has no more and no less **moral** significance than a body massage.

My erstwhile Paper on Voting

See **Ex Cathedra XXIV # 74**

I am tempted to say: the worst-behaved children in the world are American ones.

Die Welt von Gestern

Why this title keeps rolling over in my brain, over and over again, and every so often comes sputtering out, and then back and over and over again…

I haven't the faintest idea.

I, too, am an idolater.

I worship **The Atlas** and **The Globe**.

Sometimes I think about the fact that all these celebrities, ministers, Prime Ministers, billionaires, CEO's, idols and performers…

all have bowel movements.

I sometimes entertain myself with the thought of there being aliens **so** vastly superior, **so** far far more technologically advanced, that they are beyond the bounds of comprehension.

Even though I have always aspired to be the Planetary Dictator, the truth is that I would probably become **paralyzed** when the time came for difficult decisions.

124

I've always loved heavy rain.

(It quickly puts me in a contemplative mood.)

125

There are times when I want to disown everything I've said.

Donald Trump, 2015

This would be a joke, if it weren't for real.

127

What is it about a mangrove swamp that I cherish so much?

I have finally realized (now that it's too late) that if you want an unstressed component of a word to be pronounced, it is preferable to use a grave diacritical mark rather than an acute one.

It's terrible not to be able to speak every other language.

I definitely **do not** like to share a swimming lane.

131

I'm beginning to think Sex is a flytrap.

I take back what I said about Marjory Stoneman Douglas.

The Balkan Wars at the beginning of the 20th Century: What a mishmash of Greeks, Turks, Bulgarians, Montenegrins, Macedonians, Serbs, Romanians. What alliances, counter-alliances, treaties, counter-treaties, battles, defeats, plenipotentiaries, liberations, naval encirclements.

133

The Greek alphabet drives me crazy with its **five** different letters or combination of letters for the simple sound of "ē."

A documentary of a train trip from Oxford, England to Scandinavia via London, Belgium, Cologne, Hamburg, ferry to Denmark, Copenhagen, bridge to Sweden, Gothenburg, Oslo, Trondheim, Fauske, Narvik, Abisko, Boden, Stockholm, and back to Oxford. No narration, just music and scenes, and the winter trees and snows rushing by the moving train.

I think I have to give it an A, or maybe even an A+.

To live in a small town in Central Florida (not the megas of Jacksonville, Miami, Orlando, or Tampa) with all the amenities and capacities of an accommodating technology (but not during the summer months) is one of the best of all possible places to live.

There's something to be said for memories

keeping you warm,
and sane.

137

The "Wounded Warrior" Images

Once again, something that makes me sick to my stomach.

Merciful God, what a host of diseases I have been spared from.

Why is it that it is so often **later** that something is understood?

There really is no reason why one should be proud of his accomplishments.

The only thing he should consider is that he's been **lucky**.

141

Quite a comedown for me: when reading **The N.Y. Times**, I even look at "Business Day" before "The Arts."

A quite good number of lawyers: vultures.

A good number of doctors: ditto.

143

Lately, all sorts of Greek words, expressions, phrases, homilies come back to me and flood my consciousness—things I haven't thought about for years.

Is this some sort of infantile reversion?

144

When I am asked to hold on, on the telephone, must I also have to listen to crappy music?

Again

I just cannot abide a documentary where the focus is on the concocter of the documentary.

A self-admiring performance.

Time to switch off.

I like it that Americans use first names for even the chanciest of acquaintances.

147

All the things I've learned, all the experiences, awarenesses, refinements, discoveries to soon be utterly discreated and extinguished.

The iconography of Ethiopia speaks to me more than any other.

149

Life, and all of its experiences, is a **single definite particular** line. Everything else and "What might have been," as Eliot said, "is an abstraction Remaining a perpetual possibility Only in a world of speculation."

Carrying my catheters wherever I go is sort of like the President and his ever closeby nuclear codes.

151

Going through life not noticing…

The greatest demerit of my life is neglect of the aesthetic.

The best jello is red jello.

I'm so tired of cathedrals, castles, ruins, Greek temples, Roman aqueducts, old fortifications, retired cannons, archeological museums, crumbled statues...

Spare me.

There is something special, peaceful, delightful about the Kerala State of India.

155

What self-respecting writer or narrator would ever use the word "picturesque"?

I wonder how many languages the Head Concierge of the Hotel Metropole in Monte Carlo speaks?

Militant atheists are as bad as their counterparts.

How **good** some things are, at just the right time and the right circumstance: popcorn, marshmallows, hot dogs, hot toddies, pumpkin pie…

Did you ever stop to think how **beautiful** a little hand-held calculator is?

Instant dislike: Senator Jeff Sessions of Alabama.

There is something **fundamentally** wrong and rootless—having to do with its very core—about American music.

I'd rather listen to **any** folk music throughout the Globe over jangly and frenetic American music.

Same-Sex Marriage

I don't see why gays and lesbians cannot enter into a partnership in which **ALL** the rights, privileges, responsibilities, and legalities afforded to married couples would apply equally to them.

"Partnership" would then become a technical term, and everyone would understand what is meant by "my partner," "I partnered with…," "I divorced my partner," I was partnered for ten years with…," "my partner and I," etc.

Why this insistence on using the word "married," which has always meant what it has traditionally meant.

As much as I have adored, worshipped other writers, it is only with one in which I feel utterly on the **inside**, inside his very entrails, and looking outward: and that, of course, is Thomas Wolfe.

165

I need to be discovered.

Oh how many culinary marvels and inspired mixings and comminglings have I missed!

The New York Review of Books

What makes anyone think he has even the slightest handle on what goes on, and what has gone on, in this immeasurable world?

The plethora is overwhelming.

The masses and masses of men and women in all the Mega-Cities: Each one a Universe, each one an inescapable Center, each one beset with all sorts of anxieties and problems.

I sometimes daydream of those vastly superior aliens taking me in their vastly superior spaceship in which we can zip instantly along and, from one instant to another and from on high, look down upon Mega-Cities and Antarctic Regions and enormous Sahara wastes and tropical rain forests and escarpments and thrusting mountain ranges and fanned-out deltas and coastal contours and uninhabited islands.

No rickshaw drivers or hamals in a civilized society.

What more stimulating and remarkable pursuit than the history of technology.

Oh how many gave their lives for all the tunnels, bridges, subways, skyscrapers, dams, railroads... to be built.

173

Like Odysseus chained to the mast, I have found a kindred way to control my drinking.

I make **a priori** judgments about empirical matters all the time, and I don't feel very sinful about it.

Two examples of quite minor gestures that soured me on the individuals involved in quite major ways:

The way Donald Trump once handed his overcoat to an underling.

The way Arianna Huffington was so flippantly scornful of people who need sleeping pills.

It's not only a matter of "Yes" or No" or "Undecided."

There are those who just don't participate in polls.

Talk show call-ins: Is this a little of everyone's fifteen minutes of fame that Warhol talked about?

Great literature has to be somewhat local and topical; otherwise it's just more of abstract (philosophical) mooing and fluff.

179

It's hard to forget Carmen Miranda.

Despite whatever nasty things I may have said about the U.S.A., there's still a lot of enormous good will in the U.S.A.

Who is the greater man: Confucius or Lao Tzu?

My God, how many times I could have been dead, or in a lot of serious trouble.

Somehow, no thanks to any heroics on my part, I made it through.

I guess it's getting somewhat dangerous to travel nowadays.

"YouTube" is a wonderful thing.

For years I was ambivalent about Alan Watts. I thought that perhaps he possessed a wisdom that had eluded me.

And then I heard the cadence of his voice.

184

But, on the other hand, don't forget what happened with Henry Miller.

After a long hiatus, how startling it is to see how severely people change when they age.

187

No matter how remote the island, flotsam and jetsam will invariably wash up on its shores.

I couldn't catch up to myself again; someone **else** will have to do from 1989 onwards...

189

Aldous Huxley and the word "carminative."

I'm afraid I too am guilty of a similar boner. As late as Cornell, I am ashamed to say, I was trying to compliment my friend Harriet Sachs by telling her that her eyes were like beautiful cesspools.

The greatest mistake I ever made in handball: when winning the first game, **not** to calmly just stand there for the second—and then go for the tie-breaker.

Despite all my education, reading, teaching, conversing, practically everyday I find words in **The New York Review of Books** that I never heard of before.

Like the word "tyro," for example.

Cabo Verde, if it hasn't been overrun, seems like a good place to visit.

192

There are all sorts of personal contradictions engendered by the last entry.

Military Schools

The bad about them outweighs the good by about 5-1.

195

Finally, after untold eons of viewings, an ad with a bit of wit and humor, and not sickenly mawkish: The Duluth Trading Company.

Dr. Benjamin Hunt; Hampton, Virginia; House Calls $3.00 a visit; 1942.

Now, there is nothing I look forward to more than my red wine at lunch, and my scotch at dinner.

I'm beginning to think silence is the ultimate wisdom.

199

Late November in Jacksonville, outdoors amidst the greenery, a Bloody Mary, and a Havana cigar.

200

The prologue and epilogue of **Trivia** are simply unsurpassable.

201

Sometimes, when the wind blows, inanimate objects begin to wiggle and behave like animate ones.

Movies

80 %—garbage; 12%—not too bad; 7.5 %—quite good; 0.5%—"works of art."

203

Sometimes I have a hard time realizing that Jules Verne was French.

Old slippers have to disintegrate before they are tearfully discarded.

205

If only people knew what mongrels they really and exactly are, it would usher in the demise of prejudice.

Just as there really is no defense against being rear-ended,

So there is hardly a defense against someone who is willing to give up his life to do you harm.

207

I really don't see much difference between the drums and Peacock Angels of the Yazidis, and the chalices and Glittery Crosses of the Greeks.

Presently, my favorite Senators are Dick Durbin of Illinois and Richard Blumenthal of Connecticut.